Peggy Parish

SHEET MAGIC

GAMES,
TOYS
AND GIFTS

FROM
OLD SHEETS

ILLUSTRATED BY LYNN SWEAT

THE MACMILLAN COMPANY, NEW YORK, NEW YORK
COLLIER-MACMILLAN LTD., LONDON

FOR
BARBARA
BROWNELL,
WITH LOVE

CONTENTS

INTRODUCTION

Most people think old sheets are only good for making dustcloths or for shining shoes. But there are all sorts of things old sheets are good for.

This book will give you some ideas for games, toys and gifts that you can make from old sheets. It may help you to think of new ideas of your own.

Old sheets are also excellent for making any number of costumes. We have not included these in this book, but you can use your own imagination to think of costumes you can make.

GENERAL INSTRUCTIONS

1. Before you start, read the directions carefully.
2. Get ready all the things you will need.
3. Use a good all-purpose glue.
4. Use tempera paints, crayons, or felt pens for decorating.
5. Always spread newspaper when you use paint or glue.
6. Wash your paintbrush well before you use another color of paint.
7. When sewing, always use small stitches.
8. When you have finished, clean up and put everything away.

BRAIDING

You will need to know how to braid for some of the projects.

1. Sew or tie three strips of cloth together at one end.

2. Always work toward the middle. Bring an outside strip across the middle strip. The outside strip becomes the new middle strip.

3. Bring the opposite outside strip across the new middle strip.

4. Continue working first from one side and then from the other across the middle strip.

5. If your braid is too short, sew or tie another strip of cloth to each strip end and continue braiding.

EMBROIDERING

Several of the projects call for embroidery. The outline stitch is an easy one to do.

1. Thread a needle with two strands of embroidery thread, knotted at one end.

2. Bring the needle up through the cloth at the beginning of a line.

3. Put the thread to the left of the needle. Insert the needle a short distance forward on the line with the point coming toward you. Bring the needle out on the line.

4. Continue doing this until you have completed the line. Remember to keep the thread always to the left of the needle.

5. Make a knot on the underside of the cloth when you have finished with that thread color.

Blindman's Buff

This game can be played indoors or outdoors.

1. Tear a piece from an old sheet to use as a blindfold.

2. Choose someone to be the "blind man" and blindfold him.

3. The "blind man" tries to catch another person. If he can identify the person he has caught, the captured person becomes the "blind man."

Whose Nose Is It?

This is a good indoor party game.

1. Hang an old sheet from the top of a doorway.

2. Make a hole in the sheet just large enough to put your nose through.

3. Choose teams.

4. One team goes behind the sheet. The members of that team take turns putting their noses in the hole, while the other team tries to identify whose nose it is.

5. Each team takes a turn. The team that identifies the most noses wins the game.

Pin the Nose on the Clown

This game is good for lots of laughs.

1. On an old sheet draw a big picture of a clown, but don't draw the nose.

2. Color or paint the clown.

3. Hang the sheet against a wall or in a doorway.

4. From another old sheet, make and color a nose for each person playing the game. Put a straight pin through each nose.

5. Make a blindfold from a piece of the sheet.

6. Blindfold the first player and turn him around three times. Then let him try to find the clown and pin the nose on it.

7. The person who comes the closest to putting the nose in the right place wins the game.

8. You can make other games this way, such as Pin the Nose on the Jack-o'-Lantern, Pin the Star on the Christmas Tree, or Pin the Tail on the Donkey.

Tug of War

This is a good game to play with a friend or to use at a party. It can be played outdoors or indoors.

1. From an old sheet, cut three long strips. Tie the strips together at one end.

2. Braid the strips and tie them at the end.

3. To play the game, make a line on the ground, if outdoors, or with a strip of sheet, if indoors.

4. Choose a partner. Each of you take an end of the braided rope. Stand an equal distance from the line.

5. Try to pull your partner across the line. The one who succeeds wins.

6. If a group is playing, choose two leaders. Then each leader chooses a team. The leaders face each other, holding the ends of the rope. The teams line up behind the leaders and each player puts his arms around the waist of the person in front of him. Then each team tries to pull the other across the line. The team which succeeds wins the game.

Bean-Bag

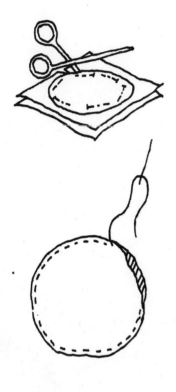

Make bean-bags to use for hopscotch and the other tossing games.

1. On paper make a pattern the size and shape you want your bean-bag to be.

2. Lay the pattern on a double layer of sheet. Pin it in place. Cut around the pattern and unpin.

3. Sew the cloth shapes together, leaving an opening for turning and stuffing.

4. Turn the bag inside out.

5. Color the bag if you like.

6. Fill the bag with dried beans. Tuck in the raw edges and sew the opening.

7. Make as many bean-bags as you need.

Target Toss

This game can be played indoors or out-doors. You will need three bean-bags.

1. On an old sheet, paint a large target.

2. Give a point value to each circle on the target.

3. Attach the target to something like a door or a fence.

4. To play the game, mark a throwing line. Let each person have three throws at the target with the bean-bags. The winner is the person who scores the most points.

Tossing Game

For this game you will need a large card-board box and three bean-bags.

1. Make three bean-bags from an old sheet.

2. Cut several holes in the side of a large cardboard box. Make sure the holes are large enough for the bean-bags to go through easily.

3. Give a point value to each hole.

4. Mark a line for the players to stand behind.

5. Each player gets three turns in trying to toss the bean-bags through the holes. The player with the highest score wins the game.

Hopscotch

This is a good indoor game for a rainy day.

1. Draw a hopscotch pattern on an old sheet.

2. Cut out the insides of the squares, leaving bars of cloth as shown.

3. To play the game, toss a bean-bag into the first square. Hop over that square and into all the others. Turn at the top and hop back. On your way back pick up the bean-bag and hop into that square as well. Then toss the bean-bag

into the second square and hop up and back. Do this with each square in turn.

4. If your bean-bag does not fall entirely in the proper square, if you step on a bar, put both feet in one square, hop in the square containing your bean-bag, or hop outside the squares, you lose your turn. The first person to complete all the squares wins the game.

5. When you have finished playing hopscotch, you can fold the pattern and save it until the next time you want to play.

Three-Legged Race

You will need to practice for this game.

1. From an old sheet, cut strips long enough to tie around the legs of two people. Cut a strip for each couple in the race.

2. Have two people stand side by side. Tie their inner legs together with a strip.

3. Practice running.

4. Mark a starting line and a finishing line.

5. Line up at the starting line. Have someone count for the race to start.

6. The couple that reaches the finishing line first wins.

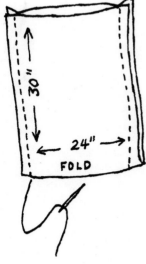

Sack Race

This game is best played outdoors where there is lots of room.

1. First you must make sacks. To do this, fold a sheet. Cut a piece 24 inches wide and 30 inches long. Let the fold be the bottom of the sack.

2. Sew each side of the sack.

3. Make a sack for each person racing.

4. Mark a starting line and a finishing line.

5. Line up at the starting line. Each racer gets into a sack and holds up the top with his hands. Have someone count for the race to start.

6. The winner is the person who reaches the finishing line first.

FINISH

PATTERNS

Mobile

You can make a mobile from an old sheet and a coat hanger.

1. On paper, draw patterns of the shapes you want to use. Cut out the patterns.

2. Lay the patterns on a double layer of old sheet. Pin them in place. Cut around the patterns and unpin.

3. Color one side of each of the cloth shapes.

30

4. On the wrong side of one shape spread a little glue. Pad the center of the shape with a bit of cotton.

5. Spread glue around the edge of the padded shape. Lay the matching shape right side up on top of the padding. Press it on the glue. Let the glue dry. Do this with each pair of shapes.

6. Trim the edges evenly.

7. Bend a coat hanger as shown.

8. With a needle and thread attach a piece of thread to each cloth shape.

9. Tie the threads to the coat hanger as shown.

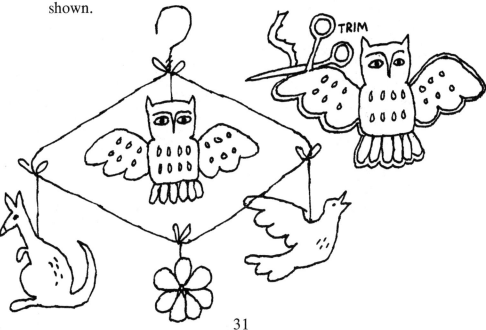

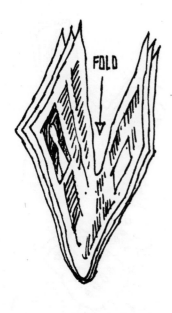

Ball in a Cone

This toy is fun to play with when you are by yourself.

1. To make the cone, you will need three sheets of newspaper folded together as shown.

2. Starting with a corner on the folded edge, roll the paper into a cone shape, and tape the edge in place.

3. Trim the top edge to make the cone about 12 inches long.

4. Put tape around the top edge.

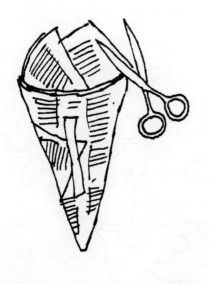

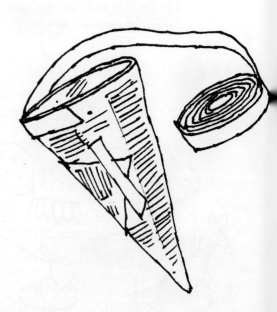

5. To make the ball, draw two circles on an old sheet, using the bottom of a glass as a guide. Cut out the circles.

6. Sew the circles together, leaving an opening for turning and stuffing.

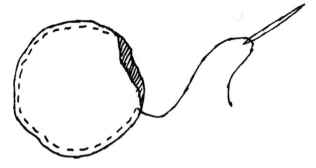

7. Turn the ball inside out.

8. Stuff the ball with cotton or with small scraps of sheet. Tuck in the raw edges and sew the opening.

9. Cut a piece of string 36 inches long. Staple or sew one end of the string to the ball. Put the other end into the

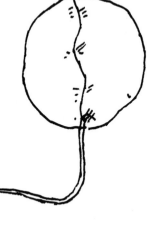

cone and staple it to the bottom of
the cone from the outside.

10. To play the game, try to toss the ball
in the air and catch it in the cone,
using only one hand.

STAPLE

Parachute

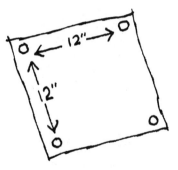

This toy is fun to use outside.

1. From an old sheet, cut a square about 12 inches long and 12 inches wide.

2. Make a small hole in each corner.

3. Cut four pieces of string, each about 15 inches long. Tie one piece of string to each corner.

4. Tie all the strings together about 3 inches from the bottom.

5. Tie the ends of the string to a small rock wrapped in a piece of sheet or to a toy soldier or small doll.

6. To use your toy, throw it as high as you can and watch it parachute down.

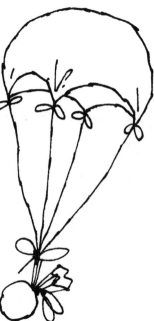

Doll

You can make a fine doll from an old sheet.

1. On paper, draw a doll the size and shape you want it to be.

2. Draw another outline about ½ inch outside the first. Cut along the outer line.

3. Lay the paper pattern on a double layer of sheet. Pin it in place. Cut around the pattern and unpin it.

4. Sew the two cloth pieces together. Leave about a 2-inch opening between the legs of the doll to allow for turning and stuffing.

5. Turn the doll inside out. Stuff with cotton or scraps. Tuck in the raw edges and sew up the opening.

6. Paint hair and a face on your doll.

Doll Dress

Your new doll will need a dress.

1. Fold a piece of old sheet so that it is wide enough to reach from the end of one arm of the doll to the end of the other arm. Cut the cloth the length you want the dress to be.

2. Starting about halfway down, sew the cloth together at the side. Turn inside out.

3. Turn under and sew a small hem around the top and the bottom of the dress.

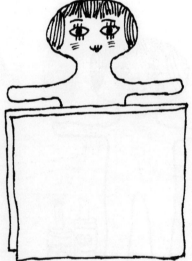

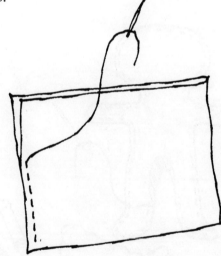

4. Arrange the dress so that the seam is in the middle of the back. About an inch from the top on each side of the dress, cut an armhole.

5. Using a needle with a double thread, sew a row of stitching all the way around the neck. Put the dress on the doll. Pull the stitching until the dress fits the neck of the doll. Knot the thread at the end.

6. Pin the dress in the back or sew on a snap if you prefer.

PULL STITCHING TIGHT

Doll Mattress and Pillow

You can make a mattress and a pillow for your doll, too.

1. For the mattress, cut from an old sheet two pieces a little larger than your doll bed. Sew the pieces together on both sides and at one end. Turn the mattress cover inside out. Stuff it with cotton or scraps. Tuck in the raw edges and sew the open end.

2. For a pillow, cut two pieces of cloth the size you want the pillow to be. Follow the same instructions as for the mattress.

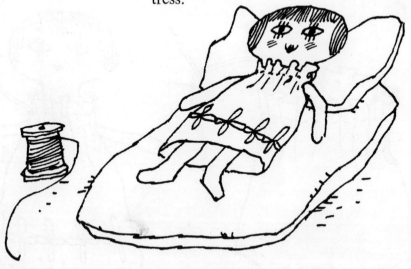

Flags

Every country and every state has a different flag. Perhaps you would like to make some flags for yourself.

1. From an old sheet, cut an oblong the size you want your flag to be.

2. Choose the flag you want to copy or make up a design of your own.

3. Crayon or paint the design on your flag.

4. You can make banners for your club or school the same way.

Stuffed Animals

You can make any kind of animal you like from an old sheet.

1. Decide what kind of animal you want to make. Draw the outline of the animal on paper. Draw another outline ½ inch outside the first. Cut along the outer line to make a pattern.

2. Lay the pattern on a double layer of sheet. Pin the pattern in place. Cut around it. Unpin the pattern.

3. Sew the two cloth pieces together, leaving an opening for turning and stuffing.

4. Turn the animal inside out.

5. You may color your animal with crayons, then stuff it, tuck in the raw edges, and sew the opening. Or you may stuff it, tuck in the raw edges, sew the opening, and then paint the animal.

Shield

With a shield, you can be a knight or an Indian warrior.

1. Cut a paper pattern the size and shape you want your shield to be.

2. Using your paper pattern as a guide, draw the shape on the side of a cardboard carton. Cut out the shape.

3. Place the cardboard shape on a piece of old sheet. Draw an outline ½ inch larger than the shape. Cut this out.

4. Lay the cloth flat. Place the cardboard shape on it. Spread glue around the edge of the cardboard.

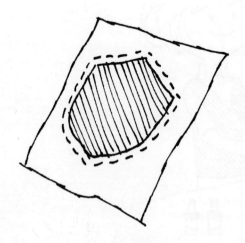

5. Pull the edge of the cloth over the cardboard. Press it on the glue. Let the glue dry.

6. Paint the shield as you like.

7. When the paint is dry, glue a piece of elastic to the center of the back as shown. Let the glue dry. Then you can carry your shield on your arm.

83414

Jewelry

You can make a necklace, a pin, and a bracelet from an old sheet.

1. Make a paper pattern the size and shape you want the jewelry to be. Keep the shape simple.

2. Lay the pattern on a double layer of sheet. Pin the pattern in place. Cut around it and unpin.

3. Color one side of each cloth shape.

4. On the uncolored side of one shape spread a little glue. Pad the center of the shape with a bit of cotton.

5. Spread glue around the edges of the padded shape. Lay the matching shape, colored side up, on top of the padding. Press it on the glue. Let the glue dry. Do this with each pair of shapes.

6. Trim the edges evenly.

7. For a pin, sew a safety pin to the back of the shape.

8. For a bracelet, sew the shape to a rubber band.

9. For a necklace, make two small holes in the shape as shown. Through the holes thread a piece of colored yarn long enough to go over your head easily. Tie the ends.

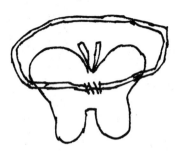

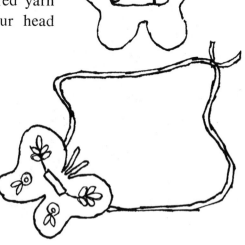

Hideout

Everybody wants to be alone sometimes. You can make a hideout with an old sheet.

1. Put up a card table.

2. Hang an old sheet over it.

3. Crawl into your hideout.

4. You can use this hideout as a cave or as a place to share secrets with your best friend.

Masks

You can make a mask from an old sheet.

1. To make a pattern, cut out a piece of paper 10 inches long and 3 inches wide. Shape as shown.

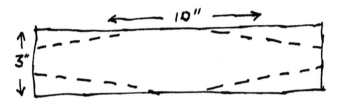

2. Lay the pattern on a double layer of sheet. Pin it in place. Cut around the pattern and unpin.

3. Cut holes for the eyes.

4. Glue the two cloth pieces together around the eyes. Then glue the pieces together around the outside edge. Let the glue dry.

5. Crayon or paint your mask if you like.

6. Sew a piece of elastic to each end of the mask as shown.

Headband

You can make a headband for your Indian games.

1. Measure around your head plus 1 inch. From an old sheet, cut a strip that length and 4 inches wide.

2. Fold the strip in half lengthwise. Sew the long edges together. Turn inside out.

3. Decorate the headband with crayons or felt pen.

4. Tuck in the raw edges and sew the ends of the strip together.

5. Staple a real feather or one cut from paper to the back of the headband.

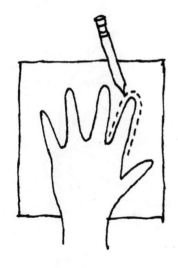

Finger Puppets

You can make finger puppets very quickly.

1. On a piece of paper draw around the end of each of your fingers. Draw another line ¼ inch outside each one. Cut along this outer line to make patterns.

2. Lay the patterns on a double layer of sheet and pin in place. Cut around the patterns and unpin.

3. Sew each pair of cloth pieces together except at the bottom. Turn each inside out.

4. Make a face and hair on each finger puppet.

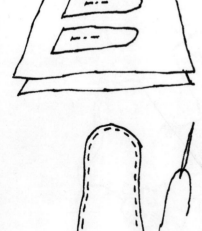

Puppet

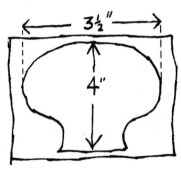

Puppets are fun to play with.

1. To make a pattern for the puppet's head, draw a line 3½ inches long. From the center of that line draw a line 4 inches long. Join the lines as shown. Cut the pattern out.

2. Lay the pattern on a double layer of old sheet. Pin it in place. Cut around the pattern and unpin.

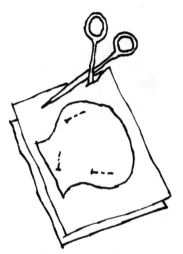

3. Sew the two cloth pieces together along the curved edge.

4. Turn the head inside out.

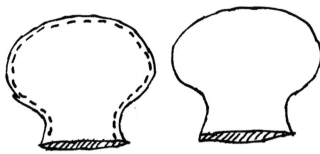

5. You can color a face on the puppet now with crayons or wait until it is finished and paint it.

6. Stuff the head with cotton or scraps.

7. Take a tube such as the ones found in bathroom tissue and cut it in half as shown.

8. Insert one of the halves into the head to make a neck. Glue the head around the tube.

9. To make a dress for the puppet, cut a piece of sheet 10 inches wide and 6 inches long.

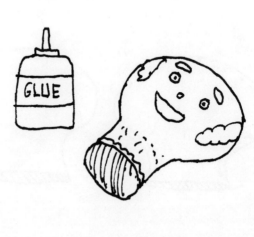

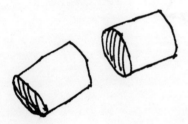

10. Sew the short ends together. Turn the dress inside out.

11. Arrange the dress so that the seam is in the middle of the back.

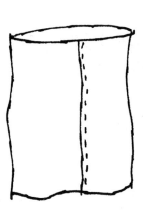

12. About an inch from the top cut a hole on each side of the dress, one for your thumb and the other for your pinky.

13. Using a needle with a double thread, sew a row of stitching all the way around the neck. Put the dress on the puppet head. Pull the stitching until the dress fits the neck. Tie the thread in place. Glue the dress to the neck. Let the glue dry.

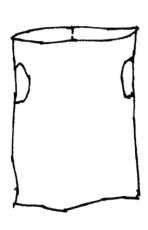

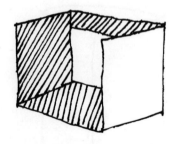

Puppet Stage

You will want a stage for your puppets to perform upon.

1. Cut the top and one side from a cardboard carton. Cut the opposite side as shown.

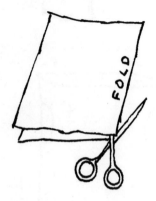

2. For the curtain, cut from an old sheet a piece 1 inch longer than the open side of the box and wide enough to cover the opening.

3. Fold this piece in half and cut along the fold.

4. Turn under a 1-inch hem at the top of each piece.

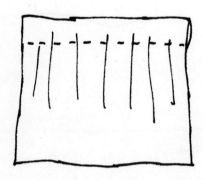
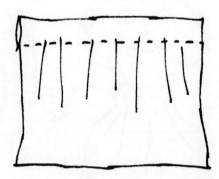

5. To attach the curtain to the stage, measure a piece of string long enough to reach across the front of the box plus 2 inches. Cut the string twice this length.

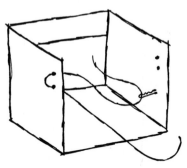

6. In each side of the stage make two small holes as shown.

7. Thread the string through the holes on one side as shown. (This can easily be done if you slip the string through a bobby pin.)

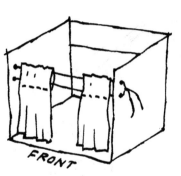

8. Thread both ends of the string through the hem of the curtain.

9. Thread one string through each hole at the other side. Pull tightly and tie.

10. You can close or open the curtains with your hands.

Drawstring Pouch

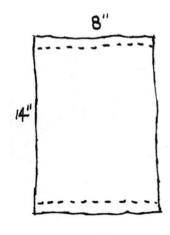

8"

14"

This pouch is good for holding jacks or marbles or other small treasures.

1. From an old sheet, cut a piece 14 inches long and 8 inches wide.

2. Turn under a 1-inch hem at each short end.

3. Fold the piece so that the hems are on the outside. Sew the sides up to the hems. Do not sew across the hems.

4. Turn the pouch inside out.

5. Cut two pieces of yarn or string, each 16 inches long.

6. Tie one piece of string around a bobby pin. Thread the string through the hem as shown. Tie the ends together.

7. Starting from the opposite side of the hem, thread the other piece of string through in the same way. Tie the ends together.

8. Pull the strings to close the pouch.

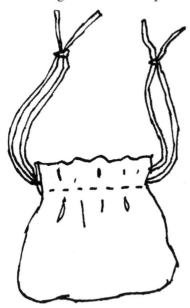

Flowers

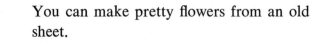

You can make pretty flowers from an old sheet.

1. Cut out a paper pattern the size and shape you want your flower to be.

2. Lay the pattern on a double layer of old sheet. Pin it in place. Cut around the pattern and unpin.

3. Spread glue on one side of one of the flowers. Place a pipe cleaner on the center.

4. Press the other half of the flower on the glue. Let the glue dry.

5. Paint the flower as you like.

Jump Rope

You can jump rope alone or with a friend.

1. Cut three long strips from an old sheet. Sew or tie them together at one end.

2. Braid the strips.

3. If the braid is not as long as you want your rope to be, sew or tie another strip to each strip end and continue braiding.

4. Sew or tie the ends together.

PICTURES

Paint a Picture

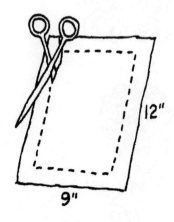

An old sheet is good for painting.

1. To make a frame for your picture, cut out a piece of cardboard 9 inches wide and 12 inches long. Draw a line about 1 inch from the outside all the way around. Cut along this line.

2. From an old sheet, cut a piece about 9 inches wide and 12 inches long.

3. Put glue around one side of the frame. Lay the cloth on the frame and press the edges into the glue. Let the glue dry.

4. Paint your picture as you like.

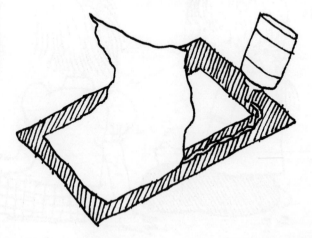

Embroider a Picture

You can make a very pretty picture with embroidery.

1. From an old sheet, cut a piece about 9 inches wide and 12 inches long.

2. Draw a picture on the sheet. Keep it simple.

3. Embroider your picture.

4. To make a frame for your picture, cut out a piece of cardboard 9 inches wide and 12 inches long. Draw a line about 1 inch from the outside all the way around. Cut along this line.

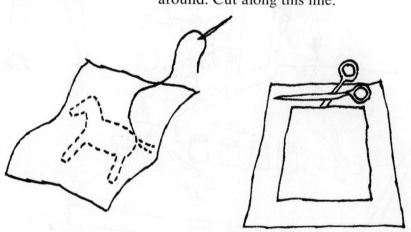

5. To frame your picture, put glue around one side of the frame. Lay the cloth on the frame and press it into the glue.

Roller Movie

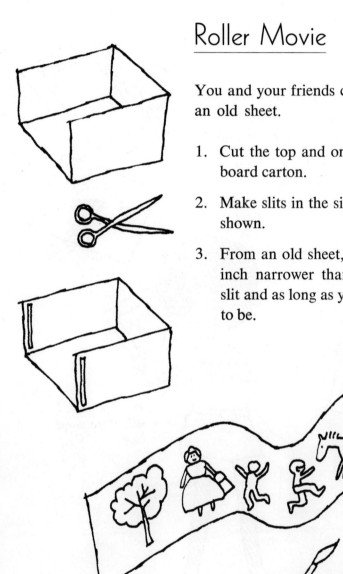

You and your friends can make movies on an old sheet.

1. Cut the top and one side from a cardboard carton.

2. Make slits in the sides of the carton as shown.

3. From an old sheet, cut a strip about 1 inch narrower than the height of the slit and as long as you want your movie to be.

4. Crayon or paint your pictures on the cloth strip.

5. Glue the end of the strip to a paper towel tube. Let the glue dry.

6. Wrap the strip around the tube.

7. Thread the strip through both slits in the carton. To make the movie move, pull the strip slowly through the slits.

Baby Book

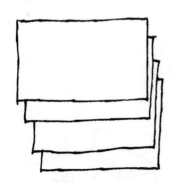

A cloth book is the best kind for a baby.

1. Decide on the size you want your book to be.

2. From an old sheet, cut four pieces of cloth the height you want and twice the width.

3. Lay the pieces one on top of the other and sew them together down the middle.

4. Fold the book.

5. Crayon a picture on each page.

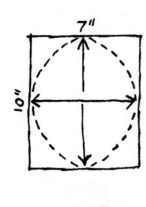

Baby Ball

Make a cloth ball for a baby you know.

1. To make a pattern, draw a line 10 inches long on paper. Bisect it with a line 7 inches long. Join the lines as shown.

2. Cut out the paper pattern.

3. Lay the pattern on a triple layer of old sheet. Pin the pattern in place. Cut around the pattern and unpin.

4. Sew the three cloth pieces together as shown. Leave an opening for turning and stuffing.

5. Turn the ball inside out. Stuff with cotton or scraps. Tuck in the raw edges and sew the opening.

Pocket Apron

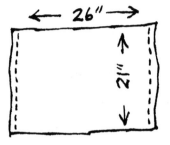

This is a good gift for your mother or a favorite aunt.

1. From an old sheet, cut a piece 26 inches long and 21 inches wide.

2. Turn under a narrow hem along the short sides.

3. Turn under a 2-inch hem along the top to make a casing for a drawstring.

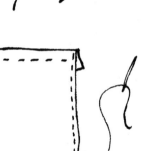

4. Turn *up* a narrow hem at the bottom, turning it in the opposite direction from the hem at the top.

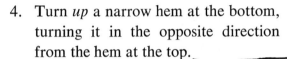

5. Fold the bottom 5 inches up on the front of the apron. Sew each end in place.

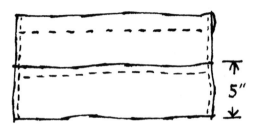

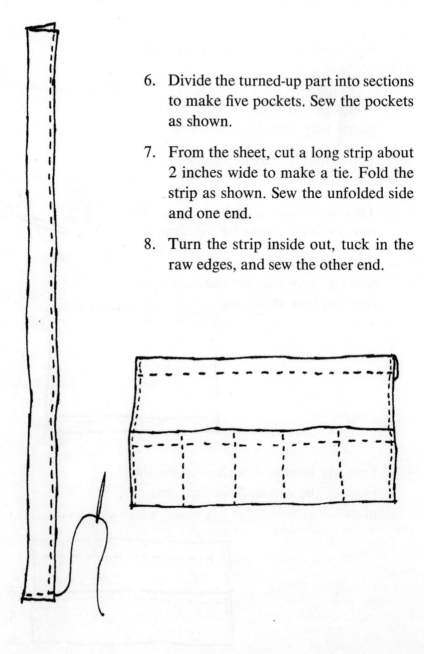

6. Divide the turned-up part into sections to make five pockets. Sew the pockets as shown.

7. From the sheet, cut a long strip about 2 inches wide to make a tie. Fold the strip as shown. Sew the unfolded side and one end.

8. Turn the strip inside out, tuck in the raw edges, and sew the other end.

9. Pin one end of the tie with a large safety pin. Push the safety pin into the casing at the top of the apron and thread the tie through.

10. Remove the safety pin. Pull the apron along the tie until it is gathered the way you want it.

Decorative Pillows

Make pillows to decorate a bed or the sofa.

1. On paper draw the size and shape you want your pillow to be. Cut this out to use as a pattern.

2. Lay the pattern on a double thickness of sheet. Pin the pattern in place. Cut around the pattern and unpin.

3. Sew the two cloth pieces together, leaving an opening for turning and stuffing.

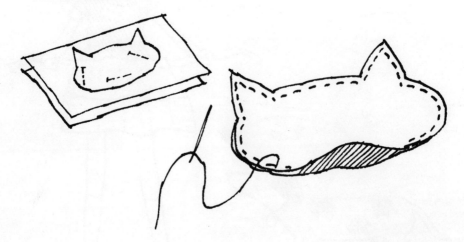

4. Turn the pillow inside out.

5. Decorate the pillow with crayon or felt pen.

6. Stuff the pillow with cotton or scraps. Tuck in the raw edges and sew the opening.

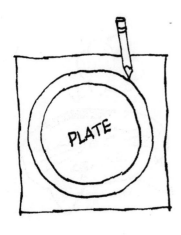

Hot Roll Basket

This makes a good gift.

1. On a piece of paper, make a circle by drawing around a dinner plate. Cut out the circle.

2. Lay the paper circle on a triple layer of old sheet and pin it in place. Cut around the circle and unpin.

3. Make a small hem around the edge of each cloth circle.

4. If you like, trim the edges of each circle with rickrack.

5. Draw lines on one circle as shown.

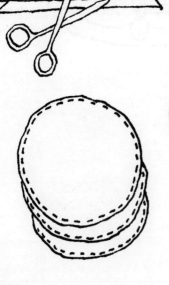

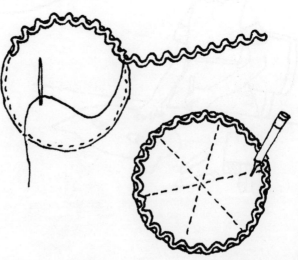

6. Join two circles together by sewing along these lines.

7. Put the third circle under the two that are joined together. Join it to the middle circle as shown.

8. You will need two snaps. A snap has two parts. The thin part is called a stud. The part that the stud fits into is called the socket. Sew the snaps on the top circle as shown.

9. Snap the studs into the sockets to form pockets for rolls.

TOP

BOTTOM

STUD

SOCKETS

STUD

Pin Cushion

A pin cushion is an easy gift to make.

1. Make a paper pattern the size and shape you want your pin cushion to be.

2. Lay the pattern on a double layer of old sheet. Pin it in place. Cut around the pattern and unpin.

3. Sew the two cloth pieces together, leaving an opening for turning and stuffing. Turn the pieces inside out.

4. Stuff with cotton. Tuck in the raw edges and sew the opening.

5. Trim your pin cushion with lace or rickrack if you like.

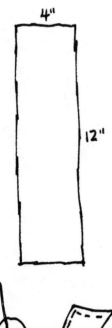

Hairbands

You can make as many hairbands as you like from an old sheet.

1. Cut a strip 12 inches long and 4 inches wide from an old sheet.

2. Fold the strip lengthwise. Sew one end and the unfolded side.

3. Turn the hairband inside out, tuck in the raw edges, and sew the other end.

4. Use crayon or felt pen to make a design on the hairband.

5. Attach a strip of elastic to the ends of the hairband as shown.

Sachet Bags

Sachet bags make clothes smell nice.

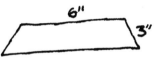

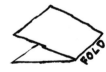

1. From an old sheet, cut a piece 3 inches wide and 6 inches long.

2. Fold the piece in half. Sew the sides together. Turn inside out.

3. Decorate the bag with crayon or felt pen if you like.

TURN INSIDE OUT

4. Fill the bag with sachet powder.

5. Sew the top opening.

6. Sew a loop of ribbon or braid on the top so the bag can be hung on a coat hanger.

Book Satchel

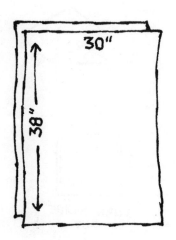

Make a book satchel from an old sheet.

1. Cut out two pieces of cloth 38 inches long and 30 inches wide.

2. Fold each piece in half lengthwise. Lay the pieces one on top of the other with the folds together.

FOLDS

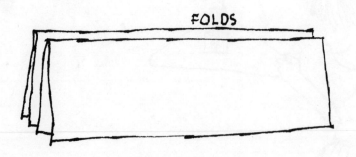

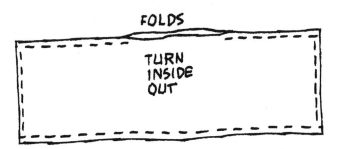

FOLDS

TURN
INSIDE
OUT

3. Starting on the folded side about 10 inches from the end, sew the pieces together as shown. Turn inside out.

4. Decorate your book satchel with crayon or felt pen if you like.

5. Then put your books in your book satchel and carry it across your shoulder.

←BOOKS→

Shopping Bag

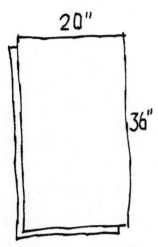

A shopping bag is a useful thing to have.

1. From an old sheet, cut two pieces, each 20 inches wide and 36 inches long.

2. Sew the two pieces together at each end. Turn inside out.

3. Fold the pieces in half as shown. Sew the side seams. Turn inside out.

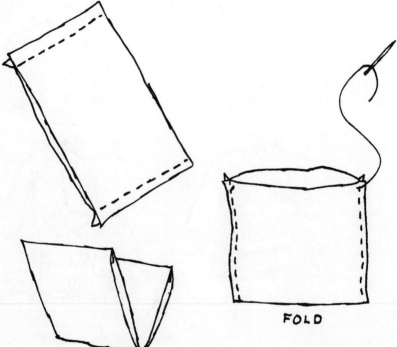

FOLD

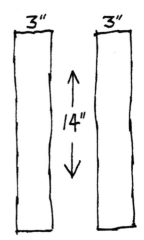

4. For the handles, cut two pieces 14 inches long and 3 inches wide from the sheet.

5. Fold each piece in half lengthwise. Sew one end and the unfolded side of each. Turn inside out, tuck in the raw edges, and sew the other end.

6. Sew the handles to the bag as shown.

7. Decorate your shopping bag with crayons, felt pen, or embroidery.

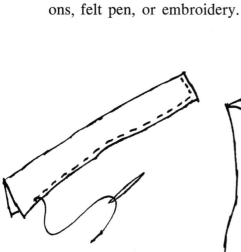

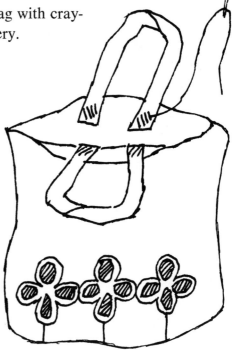

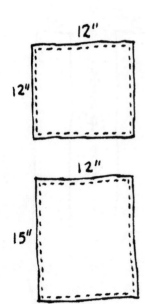

Chair Tidies

Tidies help to keep a chair's arms and back clean. You can make a set from an old sheet.

1. For the arms, cut two 12-inch squares from an old sheet.

2. For the back, cut a piece 12 inches long and 15 inches wide.

3. Turn under a small hem on all sides of each piece.

4. Embroider a design or draw a design with felt pen on each piece.

5. Trim the tidies with lace or rickrack if you like.

Bookmark

Your father might like a bookmark made from an old sheet.

1. Cut a strip 4 inches wide and 6 inches long from an old sheet. Fold the strip in half lengthwise.

2. Sew one end and the unfolded side.

3. Turn inside out, tuck in the raw edges, and sew the other end.

4. Decorate your bookmark with crayons or felt pen.

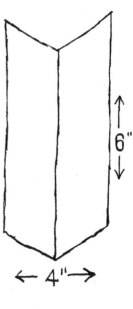

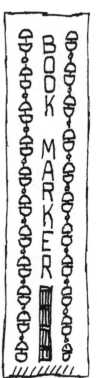

Place Mats

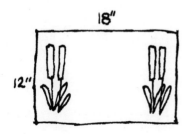

Almost everybody uses place mats.

1. For each mat, cut a piece 18 inches long and 12 inches wide from an old sheet.

2. Turn under a narrow hem all the way around.

3. Make as many place mats as you need.

4. Decorate your place mats with felt pen or embroidery.

Dresser Scarf

Many people like to cover the top of a dresser with a scarf.

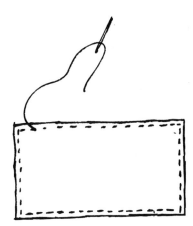

1. From an old sheet, cut a piece the size and shape you want the scarf to be.

2. Turn under a small hem all the way around it.

3. Decorate your scarf with felt pen or embroidery.

4. Trim the scarf with lace or rickrack if you like.

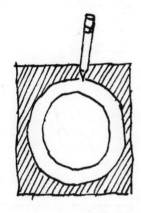

Hot Mats

Hot dishes need hot mats.

1. On cardboard make a circle by drawing around a small plate. Cut out the circle.

2. Lay the cardboard circle on a piece of old sheet. Draw around it. Draw another circle ½ inch larger than the cardboard. Cut along the outer line.

3. Lay the cardboard circle on the cloth circle. Spread glue around the edges of the cardboard circle. Pull the edges of the cloth circle onto the glue. Let the glue dry before you use your hot mat.

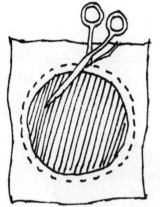

Laundry Bag

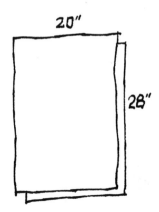

This bag would be useful for holding laundry or for storing the toys and games you've made from old sheets.

1. From an old sheet, cut two pieces, each 20 inches wide and 28 inches long.

2. Turn under a 3-inch hem at one short end of each piece.

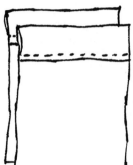

3. Sew the sides and the other short end of the pieces together. Do not sew across the hem. Turn the bag inside out.

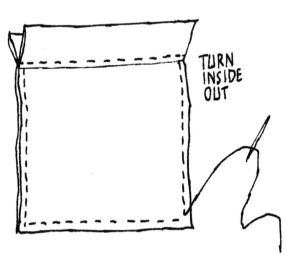

TURN INSIDE OUT

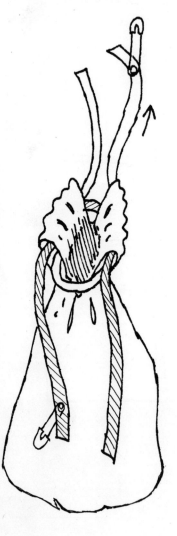

4. Cut two pieces of bias or twill tape, each 50 inches long.

5. Put a safety pin in one end of one piece of tape. Thread the tape through the hem all the way around. Tie the ends together.

6. Starting from the opposite side of the hem, thread the other piece of tape through in the same way. Tie the ends together.

7. Pull the strings to close the bag.

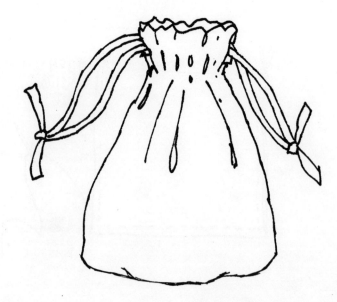